Love On Your Rank in God

Volume 1

You're Too Powerful To Love Low

Markeida Faithe, LICSW

The Power Pusher

This book or parts thereof may not be reproduced in any form, stored in a retrieval system, or transmitted in any form by any means — electronic, mechanical, photocopy, recording, or otherwise — without prior written permission of the publisher, except as provided by The United States of America copyright law.

Unless otherwise noted, all Scripture quotations are taken from the Holy Bible: New Living Translation, copyright © 1996, 2004, 2015 by Tyndale House Foundation. Used by permission of Tyndale House Publishers Inc., Carol Stream, Illinois 60188. All rights reserved. New King James Version®. Copyright © 1982 by Thomas Nelson. Used by permission. All rights reserved. THE HOLY BIBLE, NEW INTERNATIONAL VERSION®, NIV® Copyright © 1973, 1978, 1984, 2011 by Biblical, Inc.® Used by permission. All rights reserved worldwide. Copyright © 2022 Markeida Faithe

ISBN: 978-1-7368604-9-6

Dedication

I would like to dedicate volume one to my god-daughter, Addison Grace Reese. Auntie loves you and declares over your life that you will never walk through the hard things your mother and I did. I pray that you will never love, accept, or choose low in any aspect of your life. May you always move with confidence, grace, and wisdom.

Sweetie, you have a beautiful tribe cheering you on as you grace your way through life. We are here to instruct, guide, and hold you accountable so you do not later contend with a broken inner child. We will do our job even when it makes you uncomfortable. Addison, tilt your beautiful head of tresses forward and be crowned Abba's Princess, who will one day blossom into one of Abba's most beloved Queens.

TT, Faithe

Table of Contents

Introduction 1

Chapter 1: How Did I Get Here? 7

Chapter 2: Safety In The Multitude Of Counsel 15

Chapter 3: Did I Miss God? 21

Chapter 4: Loving Below Your Rank In God 29

Chapter 5: I Always Chose Low 36

Chapter 6: Your Rank In God 45

Chapter 7: It Costs to Rank Higher 55

Chapter 8: Relationship & Intimacy 57

Chapter 9: Yes To The Call 63

Chapter 10: Self-Love 69

Chapter 11: That Girl's On Fire 76

Chapter 12: You Are Kingdom 81

Chapter 13: Trade Your Cross For Your Crown 84

Introduction

There are thousands of articles, blogs, and books written for women instructing them how to position themselves to snatch their prized men. Ironically, there are just as many male relationship coaches as there are female coaches who are eagerly waiting to offer their novice and self-proclaimed expert guidance. I am not insinuating that men can't counsel and inspire women. However, I find it interesting that so many are aggressively weighing in on relational issues that affect women instead of focusing on relational issues that affect them. There is a famine in the land regarding literature offering relational guidance and accountability for men. For whatever reason, everybody wants a piece of the vulnerable female pie, and their clients are as numerous as the sands of Myrtle Beach.

On the other hand, with all of the knowledge floating around, one would think it would be enough to solve every woman's quest for wholeness and relational success. I mention wholeness because many women, and powerful women at that, believe their wholeness is attached to having a man in their lives. Not long ago, I was one of them. Sadly, even with all of the relationship literature available, there is a problem that only a few have touched on. Numerous women search for love before healing from childhood traumas and falling in love with themselves and God. Thus, they are incomplete while searching for settlement. Although they are developmentally mature, many harbor a broken inner child who desperately needs therapeutic attention. Dating and marriage for unhealed and incomplete women can prove to be disastrous and destiny-altering. This is because their unhealed inner child (when in control) dates and chooses their partners through a lens of brokenness and internal fragmentation versus wholeness.

Many women snag and hold on to men they don't feel loved, honored, or respected by. They are boxed in with men they don't enjoy, and even if they "secure the ring," they search for more after the fairytale wears off. They later awake to the realization that their broken inner child drove them into the arms of men that God never approved of, and their souls found no lasting satisfaction in.

It is no secret that most women are hopeless romantics. A deep, throbbing desire to find love and settle down is at the core of our souls.

Introduction

That's how God created us. However, the unhealed and incomplete woman contends with and succumbs to drama and disappointments far more easily than the woman who understands her value through who she is in God. The woman who understands her value through Christ pays the price to coach her broken inner child into a place of wholeness.

I apologize in advance because this series does not offer ten steps to finding a husband or getting booed up within twenty-one days. This series is your healing manual designed to awaken you to the broken imprints in your subconscious. Imprints that naggingly interrupt your ability to attain wholeness and climb higher in life and God. This is your guide to highlighting the importance of working to heal before you deal. This series will challenge you to lay to rest all soul offenses challenging your emotional progression and find beauty in the essence of who you are. It is also designed to uncover and destroy any generational warfare cluttering your path to exuding and attracting wholeness.

Sis, you can exhale because this series does not let men driven by their inner boy off the hook. We carefully examine the roles that they play in our lives. They either show up as kings or broken princes. Sometimes, just as it is for women, the representation is interchangeable. In the spirit of transparency, I share with you the relational breaking point that catapulted me into this place of knowing that there is nothing wrong with me or my desire to love and to be loved. As it did in previous seasons, it took a dramatic event where the Holy Spirit could use my pain to introduce me to my next level of teaching on the inner child. I now know that my inner child's health leads to relational wealth. Let's face it: just like me, you're too powerful to love low.

*Love On Your Rank In God … You're Too Powerful To Love Low

To change how you choose love and who you attract, you must ascend higher than the challenges of your past and modern-day culture. However, when it comes to love, if a woman is not emotionally well and aware of her rank in God (which should be every Christian woman's foundation), she risks finding herself in situations where she chooses men who are well below her rank in God. Why? Because she's unaware of her rank. In this volume, I explore how to identify and increase your rank from private to Kingdom.

*Love On Your Rank In God … Healing Your Wounded Inner Child

This volume is for the queen in you, who the unhealed child is stifling. In this volume, I paint a clear picture of the harm the broken inner child can incur when she's driving. I explore eight ways the fractured inner child sabotages the grown woman. I also raise awareness regarding how men from your formative years subconsciously build your tolerance for future relationships. Perhaps you choose lovers as you do because dysfunction is all that you know.

*Love On Your Rank In God ... Healed King, Wounded Prince

In this volume, I explain how to recognize when you are dealing with the king in him versus his broken prince. I further explore the various low offers that men make when their inner child (broken prince) is in the driver's seat. Often, we don't know how to identify dysfunction that flows from men. This volume will introduce you to game that will better help you identify offers and behaviors that will decrease your rank in God if accepted.

*Love On Your Rank In God ... Breaking Bloodline Delay & Love Limitations

This volume explores the fact that dark forces fight the forces of light to ensure that many never reach their marital pinnacle. Often, we address marital delay in the natural while neglecting what's occurring in the spirit realm. I further explore how dark powers manipulate dreams and what they can't manipulate in the natural. Lastly, I expose how they even use men of the cloth to defile God's daughters and to prevent God's sons from rising in the realm of the spirit. I also walk you through the steps to break a soul tie with the enemy to your destiny.

From my heart to yours, this masterpiece is your guide to healing thoroughly so that you can attract and choose love according to your rank in God. Simply put, you're too powerful to love low.

Markeida Faithe, LICSW

How Did I Get Here?

It is said that every woman has a breaking point, a point in time when she comes face to face with weight that she can no longer carry and breaks. At her breaking, if required, she will walk away from fine houses, cars, careers, family, and lovers whom she never thought that she could live without. She will give up everything for the cause of freedom and rebuild from scratch with zero cents to her name. When a woman is fed up, embracing the power of faith, there is no stopping her from putting it all on the line. The belief that greater is ahead and not behind fuels her to press on even if all odds are against her. Ask me how I know! Ha! I had a breaking point experience that gave me the courage to walk away from a man I loved very dearly. He was everything that I believed I needed and deserved in a man until he humiliated me. He found my breaking point on a cold, rainy October night in Birmingham, Alabama.

The Unpardonable Shoe Sin

While seated in the backseat of a stranger's car the entire drive home, I wrestled internally to answer one question, "How did I get here? I'm too valuable and powerful for this." I numbly listened to the man I adored, respectfully and attentively engage the driver as if I did not exist. I longed for him to engage me in such a manner. Instead, he appeared unbothered that I was hurting from his earlier insult that humiliated me. The insult was so unbelievable; it felt like an out-of-body experience. If experience was the most significant predictor of behavior, no apology, humility, or remorse was coming. So, in that tiny space of time, I refused to cry or fight further. Wisdom guided me to take advantage of the ride back to where we were lodging and plan my exit. And that's exactly what I did.

Although it was almost two o'clock in the morning, as soon as we parked, I went straight into his sister's house and packed my things to leave. I wish I could report that he tried to stop or block me from leaving. I wish I could say that he humbled himself and apologized or, at the very least, attempted to remedy the offense. Instead, as it was his custom, he sat and pridefully allowed greatness to walk out of his life. He played the victim when I stood up to his shenanigans. In his world, standing up to him meant that I was disloyal and a drama queen. Honestly, why should he have taken my leaving seriously when I always went back, even when he wasn't pursuing me? Out of anger and numbness, an inner truth escaped my heart and lips, and I mumbled, "I don't want you." I later blamed my flesh for saying something so brave and heartless, but I now know it was my spirit man releasing. I didn't have a holistic understanding, but I knew this breakup would differ from the others.

I didn't say goodbye to him, and he didn't say goodbye to me. He casually trailed me to the door to lock up after my departure. I heard the garage door slide down. I refused to look back. While making my way to my car, unprovoked praise erupted from my belly, which surprised me. I later came to understand what it truly meant. It wasn't until I was miles away that I had to face the pain that a call from his number wasn't going to startle my cellphone. Although leaving was the right and honorable thing to do, a storm of tears fueled by my inner brokenness violently slapped my face. Before judging me, consider this: have you ever loved someone deeply and wanted them to fight for you as you did for them? Whew! You may not understand, but Brandy most certainly does. Her song, "Have You Ever?" was written for me. If you can relate, you can genuinely imagine my pain, once again realizing that, in his eyes, I wasn't worth the fight. Desperate, I called one of my male friends, but he was too tired to talk. I texted Jamonica, my sister and mother of a beautiful newborn, my godchild. I seriously didn't expect her to be awake at such an ugly hour in the morning. However, baby girl must have known that I truly needed her, and within minutes, my cell phone rang. I recounted how my feet were swollen after standing and walking from event to event for most of the evening.

I articulated that I requested my man's socks so I could gracefully make it to the car. After all, he was the one who pointed out that my feet were swollen. Recognizing such, I believed he would have been eager to rescue me. I did not doubt that he would gladly make such a sacrifice for me, considering that I was his baby— the woman he chose to take off of the single's market. Surely, he weighed my time and effort into getting dolled up for him. I wanted him to be proud of having a beautiful and accomplished woman in his arms. I was flat-out wrong. I underestimated his brand of selfishness.

Ladies, I will admit that I committed the unpardonable shoe sin and slid my shoes off for relief without counting the cost that my beautiful shoes would rebel against sliding back onto my plump feet. I didn't know what to do, but I got the idea to ask my love for help. "Babe, can I borrow your socks?" was my simple request. To my amazement, he denied me his socks. Not only did he deny me his socks, but he also took no issue with not offering a better or lesser solution. I tried to bargain with him about the seriousness of my request, but it seemed that my voice irritated him, so I backed off. I was confused and assumed he had to be joking because, just minutes before my request, THIS WOMAN lovingly held his head upright in my hands as he nodded off to sleep in public. I did not want anyone laughing at my man, so I proudly covered him. Regardless of my honor to cover my sweetie, the honor was not mutual.

He Should Have Never Known My Name

And there I was, that DesChamps girl, The Power Pusher, Minister Faithe, Deliverance & Inner healing Minister, LICSW toting Social Worker, but more importantly, daughter of the King of Kings and Lord of Lords walking barefoot on nasty, cold, and wet pavement while watching my man walk ahead of me as if he was ashamed of me. I was so overtaken with disappointment and anger that I picked up my pace, and once I caught up to him, I asked him if he was truly that hateful. Straight-faced, he responded, "No one told you to take your shoes off, so you are getting what you deserve." By this time, I was in "Are You Serious?" shock and responded, "So, I'm just being dramatic and walking without shoes for no reason?" And he barked, "Yes, that's exactly what you are being, dramatic!" I was so embarrassed and hurt that I dared not look around me because I didn't want anyone to see my face and just how humiliated and embarrassed I felt. I dreaded the thought of encountering anyone familiar. As we finally exited the street and walked into the garage area, I looked up at him before entering the elevator and stated, "I don't have to take this. I'm worth more than this."

Once again, I tried to strike up a conversation in the car, but the car's owner quickly shut the conversation down, which was her prerogative. My soul cried louder, *"How did I get here?"* She demanded answers I did not yet have or didn't want to face. What I did know was that I deserved better treatment than what I was experiencing. I refused to hang around for the remainder of the weekend and pretend that everything was okay. I became convinced he didn't deserve to have me in his life. Sounds great, right? Ha!

I wish I could tell you I didn't contact him in the following days and weeks. I wish I could say I secured my pride and didn't beg him to take me back. I wish I could tell you that I didn't belittle myself by allowing him to disrespect me further with his tone and choice of words regarding my decision to defend my honor. I wish I could tell you I stopped reaching out despite his infamous silent treatment weapon. The number of texts, emails, videos, and telephone calls rose to an embarrassing all-time high. I cried enough tears to fill the Mississippi River and couldn't eat for days. I spent weeks blaming myself internally for asking for his socks and standing up for myself at other times during our relationship. I argued with my anointing. I became upset with my peculiar swag because it seemed that peculiar women were no longer winning. I tortured my mind with thoughts of why I complained when he had me in environments that didn't reflect who I am in God. Why did I complain about being exposed to foul language and his ratchet choice of music? I ran myself through the enemy's guilt boot camp! I partnered with the enemy of my destiny and accused myself of not being hip, sexy, skinny, or worldly enough!

I pondered: did I need to beat my face with makeup and rock some weave? Was it kinky and perverted sex that I needed to deliver? Did I need to decorate my speech with profanity and act ratchet? Was I too dark or suddenly not intelligent enough for him? I wanted to know the magic formula that would have caused my man, who I loved and covered for so many years, to respond to me like the queen I knew myself to be but couldn't reach. I needed to know what I could do to inspire him to lovingly hold me as he did the woman in the video of betrayal on his cellphone.

I was ashamed of my response to his rejection but couldn't help myself avoid craving his affirmation and validation. That happens when you've hit your breaking point, but your level of brokenness cannot sustain it. It occurs when the unhealed inner child wars with the woman within. This also happens when familiar spirits are hellbent on preventing your ascension above the parameters set for your bloodline. If only I could turn back the hands of time and operate with the knowledge I have now, he would have never known my name.

Safety In The Multitude Of Counsel

In those crushing and suffocating weeks following the offense, I opened up to my friends like never before. I needed my support system. I shared experiences I had been protecting because I didn't want to paint him negatively. After all, "love covers a multitude of sins" (1 Peter 4:8). True, but brokenness and ignorance covers abuse and disrespect. I knew that if I was going to survive and heal, I needed to be honest and vulnerable. I allowed my circle to help me carry the burden. A pastor friend and his wife spent hours on the telephone listening to my pain and pouring into me. They highlighted where I was right and where I was wrong. They asked hard questions that forced me to confront my unbalanced mindset regarding this man's presence in my life. Alex, Ryan, and Sabon gave me the rawest of rawest, using the most colorful language possible in their effort to break down what I was dealing with as men who had seen, done, and heard it all. Amid their realness, I knew they thought highly of me and wanted me to think the world of myself so I could move on and close such a painful chapter.

I was always careful to tell both sides of the story. I left no details out for the sake of making myself look good. From childhood, I was programmed to receive criticism as a norm and was indoctrinated to blame myself for everything. That stinking thinking kept me in many situations that were not worth my time or attention. Nevertheless, my sisters, Jamonica and Vicki, allowed me to vent repeatedly without passing judgment. They all drove the point home that my expectations were not too high and drilled into my psyche the price that a man truly in love is willing to pay for a woman. Although their description was one that I had never experienced before, I believed them. They built this broken woman of God up. They broke the chains, whispering to my mind that I needed to be perfect to attain loyalty, unconditional love, and respect. My son, Tyler, reminded me I was not losing anything by losing my relationship with my ex. My friend Nicole offered to come and sit and cry with me while eating ice cream. Angelica turned down her plate on my behalf and asked God to transfer my pain to her. WOW! Joyce coached and poured into me like a mother would her child. Melissa reminded me that she was praying for me as she helped me process my pain and process through my dreams that included him. It took the village rallying behind and around me, painting a clear picture, for me to see that I was carrying a weight that God never intended me to have. I gained muscle mass in areas of my life where God never meant for me to. Hear me when I say relational pain should be a foreign experience.

I was always the fighter and restorer in the relationship. Out of all my years of loving him, he never came for me during a breakup, no matter who was at fault. He struggled with apologizing and humbling himself. He had no mentors or accountability. Therefore, he did what appeased his brokenness. During every breakup, he ran into the arms of other women instead of taking a stand and pulling me closer. He took no issue abandoning me and letting me down amid commitments or transitions. Whenever I upset him, he made the path to reconciliation hell for me. I didn't know then what I now know; thou shalt not cry over a man who does not and cannot cover thee.

A friend shared a video with me regarding self-love that started a positive change in how I viewed my worthiness. I recognized that my mindset was the problem and the enemy partnered with my broken inner child in my repetitive defeat. I dug deep and mustered up the greatest "Hell NO" uttered from my bloodlines. I decided that I would see this cycle of love defeat no more! I got out of bed, put on my game face, and went outside to pray. It was midnight, but I didn't care because I meant business.

Wind of Change Blow

I took a long and hard look at my relationship history. I did not like what I saw. I was embarrassed by it all. I saw a lifetime of compromise, delay, and disappointment. I cried out to God that I needed a wind of change to blow in my life, and I meant it. I recall going outside at midnight one night and taking authority over the sun, moon, and stars. I commanded every demonic cycle of relational defeat to end in my life. I could care less who in the neighborhood heard me. I needed something from God, and I wouldn't stop until I knew He heard and answered me. I was determined never to travel that path again once He brought me out.

I decided that I was not created to cry over a man. I was not created to beg a man to love me. I was not created to become distracted by what was supposed to bring me comfort and support. I decided I was not created to send texts, emails, and videos pleading for understanding. I was not created to remain with a man who had decided that Jesus was not the son of God. I was not created to dumb down my anointing. I was not created to give my time to a man who couldn't put me first when he wasn't happy with me. I was not created to drive fourteen hours without being checked on because he was in his feelings. I was not created to be unjustly called dramatic and a liar by my lover and friend. I was not created to be the only person bringing solutions. I was not created to find unsolicited information in his cell phone. I was not created to play little girl games due to my insecurities fostered by seasons of instability and broken promises. I was not created to feel less than my beautiful self because he purposely withheld love and words of affirmation from me. I was not created to wait years for his marital covenant to be eradicated. I was not created to rock with a man who solely decided what and how much I deserved in the relationship. I was not created to teach a man how to speak, Faithe. I was not created to accept the constant excuse of his military training and age as justification to forfeit spoiling and cherishing me. I was not created to be yelled at by the man who promised to give me his last name simply because I triggered him. I was not created to excuse offenses without humility and a sincere apology. I was not created to make excuses for an emotionally underdeveloped man. I was not created to love below my rank but on my rank in God! And so it is for you. Although I was a powerful woman, I was acting and loving low.

After warring in the spirit, I went to bed and slept well. The next day, I turned my phone off and rested in God's presence until I felt a release. Ladies, He lifted the heaviness and began to speak. He reminded me that just seven days before the relationship ended, with tears running down my face, I told him I would pay the price to go to the next level in Him. Deep down in my spirit, I suspected that my most cherished love and friend would have to exit my life. I wanted to be wrong. I didn't realize that my next level ranked me higher in the spirit realm. The moment I gave God a deeper yes, not only did I receive spiritual promotion, the enemy and delay to my marital destiny had to be removed. Soon after, I left the region where I met him.

Did I Miss God?

I'm very eager to get to the end of this story, but I must share with you what held me in place for so long. I couldn't help but wonder why things fell apart when, at one point, I knew Abba approved of him. I KNOW I heard God. As I rode in the back of the car that night, I kept asking myself how I got there because I thought for sure that after a failed marriage, broken engagement, and walking through inner healing and deliverance, my relational drama was over. Readers, I need you to pay attention to what I'm conveying.

There was a time when the man who captured my heart and me was on accord. There was a time when I was very important to him, and he made me feel it by his actions. There was a time when he looked at me with such love and admiration to the point that I felt like the most cherished woman on earth. Every time I saw him, it was as if I was seeing him for the first time. My love for him ran so deep that I would have given my life for him. I'm talking about the man Abba spoke to me about in my prayers and dreams. He used to lay in my lap for what seemed like an eternity as I rubbed his beautiful bald head. He shared his innermost secrets and heart's desires with me. This man let me walk him through his first layer of deliverance and inner healing. This same man was, at one point, absolutely proud of my inner and outer beauty and uniqueness. Y'all, I'm talking about a man who attended church when I didn't and told me that once we became one, we needed to find a church home. This same man used to send me sermons to listen to and was always excited to listen to my deliverance stories and accounts of how God spoke to my heart. I'm talking about my country boy, who appreciated family, deeply loved life, and people of all diasporas. We often prayed together and talked about our desire to live for God. We talked about building wealth and creating a home where the angels of God loved to dwell. We vowed to press the reset button and save ourselves for each other. That's the man I fell in love with and would have followed anywhere. Well, almost anywhere.

Don't get me wrong, we had the usual conflict caused by unaddressed soul wounds and the merging of two cultures. However, it was nothing that the power of agreement, prayer, love, vulnerability, and humility could not overcome. We were a mess, but we both wanted change. We were on the right path to becoming a great team and believed we would eventually become one. I hear your thoughts, *"If God was truly in it, what happened?"* Hold tight! I will answer.

What Happened?

When I began to seek God, He communicated that the young man was, at one point, an excellent choice for me because he, too, was willing to give Him a yes! He, too, was the designated generational curse breaker on his bloodline and had a heart for Him. Ladies, right at the point that everything was coming together, he decided that he no longer believed in God. Somewhere along his life journey, he was exposed to layers of information that caused him to reject the Christian faith. He exercised his free will and chose to embrace the doctrines of devils. Fortunately for me, God does not keep His servants in the dark.

I was first warned in a dream but didn't understand the message. In the dream, he was talking to a woman on the telephone, and I was supernaturally added to the conversation. During the discussion, he stated, "My girlfriend believes things that I do not believe." I made a sound, and they were alerted that I was listening, and he disconnected me from the line. I awoke long enough to ask God who the woman was. I immediately drifted back to sleep and picked up where I left off in the dream. God said, "Her name is Francis, and she lives in West Virginia." The following day, when I awoke, I called him and asked if he knew of any such person, and he gave a resounding no. I believed him and dismissed the dream, and that was the end of my inquiry. I later came to realize that the woman was symbolic of witchcraft. In retrospect, there were many red flags that I decided to paint other colors.

About two months after the dream, he confessed horrible news to me one Sunday morning; ironically, the morning after, I had caught the bouquet at a friend's wedding. During our conversation, I asked why he didn't attend the prayer call I hosted. Homeboy couldn't hide his deception and snapped, "You're going higher, and I'm going lower. I don't believe in God anymore." I was rocked to my core. I yelled, "What?! You've got to be kidding me." He proudly clarified that he was not. I was so heartbroken and devastated. I cried for what seemed like months as I tried to make sense of what he communicated but could not. In my world, leaving God was unheard of. I mean, who waits until they're forty-seven years old to denounce God? I'll tell you who: a person who NEVER truly knew God relationally.

After his confession, it seemed like everything about him had changed. He always had selfish tendencies and a quick fuse, but he wanted to change and was changing through Christ. However, when he audibly renounced Jesus as the son of God, his spiritual covering was lifted, and he became more of what he had previously surrendered to

God. I was deeply grounded and wrapped up in my fanciful vision of our forever when it all unfolded. And that is how I found myself enduring his abusive behaviors that progressively got worse with time. I was still in love with the old him, the kinder and more considerate him. Suddenly, biblical truth upset him, and I couldn't keep up with what he did or did not believe. At one point, he told me that neither angels nor demons existed. He resounded that we would have known of His presence at birth if there was truly a God. He sneered that no one has returned from the afterlife to prove that God exists and that we only believe in the White man's God because our ancestors were forced to believe in Him. It was exhausting entertaining his anti-Christ rhetoric.

Those were all pseudo points of validity to the spiritually dumb, blind, and, in some instances, spiritually deceased. From out of nowhere, my love for God disgusted him. The very attribute that my tall, dark, and smexy hunk of a man once loved about me, he now despised. At one point, he broke up with me, noting that God's influence was all over me, and I couldn't hide it. I watched his moral convictions deteriorate right before my eyes. All of his spiritual convictions went out of the window. Actually, I started noticing the changes even before he admitted his truth. He became a vegan, which was great, but his speech began to change due to being influenced by a few health influencers he encountered on social media. Many of them laced their health practices with hate for

Caucasian people and promoted ancestral worship. He lost a significant amount of weight and began to look sickly. The light in his eyes left, but he bragged that his thinking was illuminated. He became obsessed with his health and, overall, less intelligent. He argued that God doesn't make anything happen for us, but we make things happen for ourselves. He later graduated to believe that there is a higher power and that he needed to send good vibes into the universe to move things in his favor—poor baby. I still tried to make it work because I was sure I heard God. I might have heard God, but I also should have listened to the scripture in Amos 3:3: "How can two walk together except they agree!"

The Cry For His Soul

My soul wanted what she wanted, and I prolonged my deception by fasting and warring for him. I entered into Christian witchcraft because I was determined to BEND his will. I wasn't so interested in his soul salvation but rather in my desire for marriage. I was concerned about what others would say and didn't want to be alone. I didn't like the pain of starting over. I couldn't help but think of the dreams, money, and time I had invested. Thankfully, I didn't stay in that place for long.

I remember when it hit me that this man was on his way to hell, and I wept and grieved for his soul. That's where Abba wanted my attention. He wanted me to focus on his soul and not my perceived loss.

He was so spiritually dead that I was left leading and fighting alone on every front. Suddenly, we had nothing in common. He was right; God was attached to every aspect of my life. He boasted that he made everything happen for himself. We quickly became an easy target for the enemy to manipulate and toy with because we were not on one accord spiritually. I tried hard to make the relationship work because I KNEW WHAT GOD SAID. However, I did not understand then that there is a big difference between what God once said and what God is now saying. There is also a difference between God's submissive versus His permissive will. My almost-man-of-God invoked his free will and said, "No thank you," to the truth that Jesus Christ is the son of God. He rejected all the benefits attached to Christ which also included me. Abba later highlighted that it wasn't his decision to entertain unbelief that disqualified him but rather his insistence to remain in error while polluting my faith in God with seeds of unbelief.

My next level YES qualified me for spiritual promotion, and his NO demoted him in the spirit and circumcised him from my life. I was released when he decided to live without Christ. However, due to my emotional investment in the relationship, I didn't perceive that God had long moved on. I outstayed my grace, which almost cost me my ministry and life. Looking back, I was beginning to die spiritually, as several of my dreams showed me. In three distinct dreams, I was revealed that he was dead spiritually, and if I remained connected to him, I would die as well. Three dreams later, I still wanted what I wanted. Readers, there is nothing like the power of a forced broken heart that will cause you to reevaluate some things in your life. What will it take to release what you know can't go with you to your next level?

Loving Below Your Rank In God

What do you do when you've lost the love of your life and have no plan B? Everything I did and imagined included this man in some manner or another— all of the time invested, the money spent, the prayers prayed, and warring in the spirit. What about the wedding colors I chose and the grand plans to make our wedding day one to remember? And no, we were never engaged. However, there was no doubt in our minds that our adventurous roads would lead us to the altar. Thoughts of his family and friends and the precious bonds we established haunted me. How about my family and friends he met and the laughter they shared with us? What about my ministry supporters praying for me to get married and anticipating meeting the man I loved? And what about all the declarations I made about breaking the anti-marriage forces operating against me and my bloodlines? So many years of waiting without fruit to show for my faith vexed me. *"Girl, you should have spread those legs WIDE,"* said my flesh! My time needs to count for something other than a testimony of *"King Jesus broke me free AGAIN."* I wanted my man, that man who was once riding with me through it all. I wanted the manifestation of my prayers and not just the grand promises of, *"God is going to do it when you least expect it."* Yes, I'm keeping it real.

Others may foolishly glorify singleness, but that is not my story. I love, love. My heart pounded at the thought of trying to get to know another man. I tortured myself with thoughts of, "Who in their forties truly has time to retell all of their glory stories and go through the process of exposing the complicated parts of their life to make themselves vulnerable?" My soul rebelled at entertaining the idea of starting over. *"It's gonna take soooo much time and energy,"* my soul bitterly shouted. My Angela Bassett, *Waiting to Exhale*, alter ego was trying to manifest. You rocked with this man for a long time, and look! My flesh yelled, *"I'm embarrassed and sick and tired of the false alarms. If you ever enter another relationship, you bet not tell a soul until the wedding day."* And, of course, every demon from hell assigned to my case was high-fiving my flesh.

One day, from what seemed like it had come out of nowhere, my flesh threw a bonafide next-level hood tantrum. She went deeper than

I wanted to go. My flesh went low. *"Faithe, this is going to be another situation where you lost a good man, and shortly thereafter, God allows him to get married in your face. Watch what I tell you. Your gawwwwd that you trust is going to allow him to flaunt his new boo in your face. He's going to give her errrthang that you wanted and then some. While you're over here trusting God, you're looking real stupid to the rest of us, watching you carry on as if your heart doesn't hurt. Is it really your portion to continue preaching, teaching, and moving about as if you do not have feelings? Girl, bye!"*

Tears started pouring with force as I entertained my flesh, speaking from her fleshly throne. I had to do something! My ego was like, "Oooooooh, so you're going to allow Ms. Flesh to talk to you like that?" My broken inner child was off in the corner crying, wondering why the loads of shame and dishonor always followed us. My spirit man said, *"Oh Lord, here we go again! I'll speak when invited."* Since I was in my feelings, I sided with those trying to derail my destiny.

Dating Dot Com Gone Wrong

There is a popular saying to get over your ex, you should find another to occupy your time. I decided to get back in the game by joining a dating site. Ha! I spent hours picking out the right pictures and writing my bio. What took so long was that I couldn't find images that made me look, you know, sexy. Needless to say, I didn't have any lust-laced photos. My phone was dry, and it had been that way for years. I figured I'd make up for it in my bio. I laid it on thick (at least in my mind). I told the dating world what I desired in a man and what I had to offer any man that came my way. Saints, I was careful to let them know that I loved the Lord and wasn't looking for a quick hookup. I was excited as I launched my Holy Ghost-blessed profile into cyberland. Hunnies, my excitement was quickly muted when my ex-husband popped up as my most suitable mate choice. Talk about dating dot com gone wrong! You're laughing, but I was livid! I IMMEDIATELY deleted my profile and cried more tears of sorrow and frustration. My flesh pouted, *"Nobody did that but the Holy Spirit. The Holy Spirit stays blocking. Someone needs to write a song about how the Holy Spirit blocks! He's a blocker; yes, He is!"*

Since my dating comeback game was an epic fail, anxiety rushed in and instructed me to run back to all of my self-soothing vices of old. Getting drunk was entirely out of the question. Masturbation could no longer satisfy me, and I refused to locate an old lover for a lovely evening. I was delivered from it all, and I was not going to return to my vomit. I thought about going shopping but my money was acting funny, so I wasn't about to spend out of control. I thought about losing myself by binge-watching a Netflix series, but the thought was not pleasurable.

I had disciplined myself to require very little entertainment. My broken inner child instructed me to drive to Calvin's residence and snatch my man back. I definitely ignored her.

I called on two old faithfuls, gluttony and self-pity. They were eager to entertain me, eager to make me smile. Eager to do some old and new tricks, yes, they are indeed versatile. And when I'm real low, they tell me so. They aim to make me feel good. They always arrive on time to make my soul climb. That day, I ate half a gallon of chocolate almond ice cream, a large meat lover's pizza, a bag of Cheetos, and a pint of strawberries. Afterward, I made sure I locked myself into the bathroom; I positioned my body in the mirror so I could witness the added effects that accompanied my ugly girl cry. And you'd better believe I gave it my all. And when I was done, guilt, condemnation, depression, loneliness, and rejection were there to rock me to sleep.

The Dreaded Holy Spirit Conversation

When I awoke, I knew I could neither afford to waste any more time drowning in self-pity nor could I continue entertaining my broken inner child while hosting conversations with demons. I automatically tried to tap into what worked for me in the past, especially during troubled waters. I decided I would reset my life and go into a deep consecration with God. It sounded like a winner to my ears, but the Holy Spirit (who quietly observed my destructive spiral the day before) nudged me past that thought. I pondered going on a resource binge. Yes, I'll read and listen to as many books and videos as possible until my spirit finds the information needed to grow past the pain I was experiencing. The Holy Spirit lovingly disagreed with that decision. I got it! I'll locate a coach and let her coach me into my victory stance. The Holy Spirit whispered, *"I am the only coach you need."*

Ladies, the Holy Spirit is neither pushy nor does He compete. As long as I insisted on entertaining conversations with my flesh, my broken inner child, and my assigned demons, He was not going to interrupt the party because I knew better. When I settled down, the Holy Spirit sternly communicated that I didn't need another resource, coaching call, or to isolate myself. He showed me I needed to accept my rank in God and stop loving low. "Accept my rank in God? Loving low? What are you talking about," was my earnest reply. I felt so vulnerable in those short moments, and my fear of rejection told me I had a rebuke coming. What the Holy Spirit said to me brought to the forefront a truth I did not want to face: I had low self-esteem residue lingering in my soul.

Shaking my head and speaking out loud, I said, "Ouch, Holy Spirit. I'm not ready to be fussed at or told just how broken I still am. I've been told all my life by mean and well-meaning individuals just how much I don't measure up." I cried out, "Have you anything good to say to me? I need a feel-good message. I need words that will build me up and bless me. What you're saying hurts, and I don't even understand it all yet. I've lost so much because of my love for righteousness, and people already think I'm weird because I'm a demon slayer. Can't you see that my life has taken a 180-degree turn since you got a hold of me in 2012? My life is quiet, and you're invited to use me anytime. Please, I told you I'll go anywhere you send me and say anything you'd like me to say. All I ask is that you bless me with a husband who loves me and God passionately." My inner child sheepishly pleaded, "You are a good woman; even *the men who walk away tell you so.*" The grown me affirmed her sentiments and added, *"And now you're about to tell me I'm the problem? I just can't. Not now. I'm already trying to pick myself up from the floor of despair. Please don't hurt me more."* My inner child echoed my heart's cry, *"Yeah! Please don't hurt us more."*

I Always Chose Low

The Holy Spirit patiently waited for His turn to speak. "Faithe, I've been waiting to have this conversation with you and all of my sons and daughters who will read the words you will one day pen. Those who read the books that I birth through you will be drawn by my spirit to do so. They will drink the words and daughter; their lives will be transformed. And because I show the ending first, please know that your God-ordained husband will read your books, and his love and drive for you will be perfected by God. Faithe, I'm not mere man. When I break someone down, it's with the pure intent of completely rebuilding them and correcting the defective parts of their lives. Your heart and prayer life invited me to come to your rescue.

"You pray dynamic prayers that demand heaven to take notice of you. Why do you think that he was never able to relocate? Why do you think he could not infiltrate your ministry? And that morning, you heard, **"I'll kill him first before I allow him to have her."** That was me speaking to what was operating in him. It had the audacity to lay claim to your destiny. Why do you think he wasn't allowed to step foot in your house but only a few times? Why do you think you could never remain comfortable with his decision to leave God? Hurt you? I was there observing everything, and so many times I wanted to rescue you, but I could not do so prematurely and without invitation. Hurt you? I blocked the fatal blows of the enemy. He tried to take you out by connecting you to a man who wouldn't be able to handle nor encompass the call of God on your life. I could have allowed you to marry him. Who do you think made him utter the truth that he didn't love the God that your mother dedicated you to? The warlock you conversed with in your kitchen told you the truth. The enemy does not care if you get married as long as you marry one of their agents.

"The enemy underestimated your love for God. Like many women, he was certain that you would choose a man over God. You would have left long ago, but he played games with your mind and used your heart against you. He encouraged you to pray when you should have released. Your prayers were so hot that they forced God to intervene on several occasions, but your lover kept choosing the path of unrighteousness. At most, the enemy delayed you but take heart, the father calculated the delay into your arrival time. You, my daughter, nor the enemy are powerful enough to cancel what God has spoken over your life even before the foundations of the earth. The man whom you call daddy has an invested interest in your life. You melted his heart when, through your tears, you prayed, **"Daddy, no matter how much I miss him and my soul calls for that which is familiar, I choose you. Even when I ask to receive him back, trump my request with your sovereign will. I no longer want to be in your submissive will but rather, your permissive will. I choose you."**

"Let me reassure you, Faithe, nothing is wrong with you. And even if there were, perfection is not a prerequisite for love. While there is nothing wrong with you, there is something wrong with how you choose those worthy of your love, time, and virtue. Because of your caring heart and wounded inner child looking for love, you cultivated a pathology of casting your pearls before swine. You love low, and you're too powerful to love low."

Low Was Ok When ...

The Holy Spirit walked up and down my life and highlighted how I repeatedly chose low men. Low was okay as long as I was not going anywhere or doing anything significant. Low was okay until I asked God for a Kingdom marriage versus a typical marriage. Low was okay as long as I didn't say yes to the call of God on my life. Low was okay when I was broken, had no hope, and was filled with rejection. Low was okay when the little girl in me was in control. Low was okay when I didn't know what God desired for me. Low was okay as long as I was a lukewarm Christian. Low was okay as long as I operated in legalism versus the freedom Christ afforded me on the cross. Low was fine when I didn't see how beautiful and powerful I was. Low was okay when I did not count myself as an asset. Low was okay before I said yes to paying the price to be the generational curse breaker. Low was okay before trading in my cross for my crown.

Prayer Did This

The Holy Spirit continued to flow. "Faithe, your prayers were bigger and more powerful than you could have ever perceived them to be. However, you prayed and believed on a MEGA level, but your vision was micro. You chose based on your current status in life versus who you would become and where God would take you. The prayers you prayed spoke to the future you, and that's why you couldn't prosper with the leveled things you chose. Your prayers blocked what couldn't hold or accommodate your destiny." He went on to express that I consistently chose men whose tents were too small to house my God rank. I tried repeatedly to fit my size fifteen feet into size five shoes. I tried to partner with those comfortable with a form of

Godliness when I wanted the heart of God. And I often did that by trying to talk them into seeking God so that they could expand their tents. I didn't realize that if I had to RAISE him spiritually to marry him, he wasn't my God-ordained spouse but, at BEST, my spiritual son. Time and time again, I tried to fit my international vision into their United States vision. I remember one man telling me that he was simple and that I was complicated. I had no idea what he meant, but it was beginning to make sense. I had another tell me that I was too heavy, spiritually, and that it would be easier (especially for a black man) to leave me for another woman who was less heavy. He was correct. I am too heavy for a man whose shoe size is five. It would be easier for him to float to a different type of woman.

In the past, I chose low because my thoughts concerning myself were low. I stood corrected. The Holy Spirit was not telling me that I had low self-esteem. It wasn't even about low self-esteem residue. I wasn't seeing far and high enough. My view of myself and knowledge of God's will for my life needed to be adjusted. In my eyes, I was just Faithe, but in the spirit realm, I am powerful and extremely important because I said, "Yes" to God and to putting in the work that elevation requires. The Holy Spirit showed me that in the spirit realm, I am ranked very high for reasons that, in all honesty, seem foolish to me.

However, it was made clear that God has very important work for me, and the wrong alignment for me, as it is for you, is a destiny killer.

The Holy Spirit conveyed that I'm too powerful to love low. Before then, I never admitted to myself or spoke out loud that I was beautiful, powerful, and much more significant than I allowed myself to be. I never allowed myself to admit that I need a grown man of God to ROCK on these arms. I need a man who is equipped to lead and cover me. I need a man of God who is not interested in changing me because he's been predestined to speak, Faithe. A man who knows my name not because he heard it but because it's embedded in his rib. Whew!

Time and time again, as a general in the spirit, I tried to partner with the newly enlisted, or heck, civilians. And so, I felt rejected, dejected, and misunderstood when, in all actuality, the men that I chose were giving me their very best based on their various levels. Looking back, I was indeed a frustration to them, and as a result, it was easy for them to feel as if they could not satisfy me or that I didn't know how just to chill and let them be. It wasn't that they didn't love me, they couldn't house me. I was the WORK, TIME, AND ENERGY; they were not emotionally or spiritually equipped to nurture. And that is why it was easier for them to quickly run to other women or marry soon after our relationship ended. They ran into the arms of women whom they were more compatible with. They ran into the arms of women whose rank they could better accommodate.

While Renee thrived in such an atmosphere, Faithe might not have felt comfortable at the club. Faithe may not have felt comfortable fornicating, while Jeanne had no such conviction. Faithe might have desired quality time and words of affirmation to feel loved, whereas Tiffany accepted that a piece of a man was better than no man. Dreya might be okay with a man who doesn't have a relationship with Christ, whereas it was a deal breaker for Faithe. I was beginning to see clearly. This was deeper than being compatible on Earth. You can be compatible with a person in the natural but not the spirit realm. In such a case, you're meant to be friends, not a couple. And oftentimes, we marry, date, or fornicate with such persons. My ex-husband will quickly inform you that he isn't interested in dealing with Faithe, the deliverance minister. Calvin never read my first book, joined my ministry pages, or attended any spiritual events I hosted. However, he never missed a chance to participate in non-spiritual functions or support me in other ways. Selectively supporting me should have been a deal breaker alone. Love doesn't fragment the focus of its attention. Love all of me or none of me is my new standard.

Reflecting through healed lens, none, and I mean none, of the men that I dated could have handled what God called me into. WOW! Mind blown! This was about me tapping into the fullness of who I am and owning it. I couldn't get high because my vision was low. Consider the headlights on a car; if they are positioned incorrectly, you will not be able to see very far ahead of you at night. As a result, you must decrease your speed or risk missing crucial turns and possibly having an accident. You also become difficult to spot by oncoming drivers. My low vision slowed me down and made it hard for me to be detected by high-ranking suitors.

Holy Ghost Physical Therapy

Near the completion of this chapter, a young lady felt impressed to send me the following text, "When someone comes into your life who is not supposed to be there, in the realm of the spirit, they cause you to wreck and lose your ability to walk out your destiny freely. Once they leave, you must enter the Holy Spirit's physical therapy program to regain destiny-changing mobility." My God! I received my aha moment! The Holy Spirit did not come to rebuke me but to raise my vision and to rehabilitate me! His visitation concerned me becoming convinced and grounded in who I truly am in God while highlighting what in my mindset needed to be reformed.

I was personally invited into the Holy Spirit's physical therapy boot camp, and guess what? So are you because you are too powerful to love low. He's invested in getting us into proper alignment to meet, love, and marry our best friend and Kingdom mate—the man who shares the same rank or, even better, outranks us. Even if he outranks us, we will be ranked high enough to honor his rank without worshipping or feeling inferior to him. I was now beginning to understand just what it means to marry up! The light was coming on in my head, and my view of myself was shifting. At that moment, I realized that my spirit man definitely whispered to the ex (like a child hiding behind their parent while talking trash to their bully), "I don't want you." The broken child in me didn't mean it, but the grown woman certainly did. The grown woman recognized that she was too powerful to love low.

Your Rank In God

We enter this world ranked equally in God but don't remain equally ranked. Our environment, understanding of God, how we process and apply the principles found in his word, and our interpretation of the many twists and turns of life are some apparent understandings that affect the expanding, elevating, or lowering of our rank. Although I am primarily addressing rank from a spiritual perspective, as it is in the natural, the higher your rank, the higher the pay and benefits attached to it. Your motivation and ability to go the extra mile can also affect the speed at which you are promoted. Satan's job is to ensure that he sends disruptions into your life as early and often as possible that will negatively affect how and if you grow in rank. Satan's job is to taint how you see and feel about yourself and God, knowing that both affect how you present yourself in life. There is no denying that there is a correlation to understanding your rank in

God that will reflect how you accept and treat yourself and others. It's equally linked to what you expect and demand from society and God.

Rank & Love

Sticking to the theme of this book, I must express that your rank in God will reflect in who you receive love from. You are too powerful to love low, but when you don't understand your God rank, it is highly probable that you will choose paths that lead to loving, thinking, and accepting low. You will confuse crumbs for the loaf and call bondage, God's will for your life. You will continue to settle for "it's complicated" type relationships and nurture soul ties that need to be severed at the root. You'll likely outstay seasons and attract lack. Because you lost sight of your actual rank, more than likely, you will entertain hinderers of your destiny primarily because you judge them in the natural while ignoring them in the spirit. When you don't know your rank, you will cry, chase after, and beg for what is no good for you. Ignorantly and carelessly, you will trade in your birthright for a right now fix.

When you don't know your rank in God, you will see your single years as your enemy versus seeing them as your friend and the opportunity to mature. You will think it's okay to disrespect and defile your body with booty calls and cuddy buddies, all in the name of, "I'm grown, and God knows I have needs." You will allow a man to string you along without solidifying you as his. You will accept shacking and promises of a ring while producing his children. When you don't know your rank, you will allow men to forcefully put their hands on you and call you out of your name without penalty. You will cry more than you laugh. You will lose yourself in his world without seeing the value of yours. You will allow married men or committed men to sell you dreams while draining you of your dignity. You'll play games for attention. You will repeat the failures of your bloodline when you're ignorant of your rank in God. Notice that I did not say rank in this world but in God. You must know your rank in God to attract and love high.

Your Rank & Self Treatment

This is the part that many believers are missing! When you don't know your rank in God, jealousy and comparison will be your portion, and you will become highly critical, dismissive, and abusive toward yourself and sometimes others. When your rank in God is not precise, you will eventually water down your dreams and morals, become bitter, and ultimately, lose yourself and die with regret.

In a world where everything is about the show, I don't want you to think for a moment that you are excluded from being ranked high in God because of what you do or do not have. Furthermore, don't fall into the trap of believing that you are ranked higher than you are or that you qualify for more than you genuinely do. I can't begin to tell you how many women post that they desire a Kingdom man but yet behave like women of the world. They may want a Kingdom man, but they do not qualify. They may qualify for a man, but their spiritual status is insufficient to attract a Kingdom man. God was serious about his counsel that we should not be unequally yoked with unbelievers.

God's Love

You may wonder how you rank and what you need to do to rank higher. How you rank and the ability to rank higher in God is based on what you believe about God and what you believe He thinks about you. Your rank increases as you put into practice His standards for your life. You must understand that God's love is the fundamental basis of your rank. You are an intelligent and sophisticated Being created by the God of the universe. It doesn't matter how you were conceived or what you've faced in life that tore you; He fashioned you on purpose and with love. You are not a mistake. His thoughts towards you are lofty. He knitted you together in your mother's womb, and you, my love, are fearfully and wonderfully made (Psalm 139:13-14). That's love, and it must be the foundational layer of your worth and rank in God. To lose sight of this truth will throw your entire life off kilter. This is why traumas of all sorts hunt you down.

The enemy knows that a life without knowing how valuable it is to God will reek of Kingdom contradictions.

I remember a young woman recounting a story from her past abusive marriage. Her then-husband was cruel. During one of his episodes of cruelty, he tied her up for days and tormented her. His ultimate expression of disrespect and disdain for her included putting a gun to her head and threatening to take her life. What gave her the strength to break free was the foundational truth that he didn't give her life and, therefore, he didn't have the authority to take it. It was the realization and enforcement of her rank grounded in God's love for her that she tapped into and demanded her freedom. Like the prodigal son, she came unto herself and gave a "Hell NO" that the gates of hell could not prevail against! I command you, woman of God, in this very moment, to come back to yourself and leave that pigpen you're dwelling in. Do you have a "Hell No" in your spirit? Then SAY SO! You are too powerful to love low.

Jesus' Death

Taking it a step further and considering the great fall of humanity as detailed in Genesis chapters 1-5, you are so important to God that He gave His son, Jesus, to die for you so that you can have life more abundantly (John 3:16). This foundational truth stacked on top of the last one we discussed should influence your view of yourself for the better. Before Jesus' sacrificial death, animals had to be slaughtered, and high priests represented the repentant in the Holy of Holies (Hebrews 13:11). Most encounters were secondhand encounters with God. Sweetie, not anymore. You have the right to go directly to God for yourself. No one has to clear the way because Jesus did it for you when he died on Calvary. You have direct access, and you're wanted in His space (Hebrews 4:16). Somebody loved you enough to die for you. Yes, you!

Woman of God, it is imperative that you pause long enough to understand that the creator of all things beneficial knows your name. He is interested in every detail of your story, how you feel, and, more importantly, where you're headed. You're not on earth unloved or unsupervised. Period. I can hear some of you groaning that you feel unsupervised when you survey your life. Maybe so, but Jesus never promised that every day would be Sabbath. He stated, "In this life you will have trouble but you must take heart because He has already overcome the world" (John 16:33). When you are in Christ, He is in you and you have access to ALL of His benefits. You are an overcomer, so it's time to act like it. In the face of rejection and abandonment, somebody loves you! So much so that they gave their life for YOU!

The Royal Family

Accepting Christ as your personal savior automatically accepts you into the Royal Family of God. You become an heir of God's wealth, meaning, as his child, all He possesses rightfully belongs to you (Ephesians 1:5). You left the slave role and entered into daughtership (Ephesians 4:7). That makes you powerful. Whether you realize it or not, you became a part of an elite family of believers with incredible Kingdom benefits. Talking about RANK in God, you're ROYALTY! Stop envying the royal family and start rocking your royal status. You are indeed too powerful to love low. You are royalty. And thanks to what Brother Jesus did, you also became a part of the royal priesthood (I Peter 2:9-10)! To put the icing on the cake, you get to call the King of the universe Abba, aka Daddy (Romans 8:15).

Many people have a hard time calling God, daddy, and father because they have daddy issues that knowingly and unknowingly trigger them. Others see God as a taskmaster type of God, so calling him daddy is somewhat offensive to their psyche. Nevertheless, when you accepted His son, you were adopted into the Kingdom of God. You went from a fearful enslaved person to His confident daughter, and He became your involved father who is interested in every aspect of your life (Romans 8:15). It is beautiful! What an incredible third foundational layer; consider it your threefold cord. When that threefold cord is intact, you cannot be easily broken, manipulated, or stopped. Are you beginning to understand why the enemy has been so eager to turn you into "damaged goods?" You're the only person who doesn't know how powerful you are.

Playing Catch-Up

Accepting that you're royalty, loved, and so important that someone died for you and entered you into royalty should boost your confidence to the maximum. Allowing anyone to mistreat and misguide you is below your rank in God. God does not make faulty investments. He modeled your worth on the cross, and you should be so fired up to enforce your worth that you dismiss anything and anyone who doesn't cultivate your value. Knowing and modeling your worth is another level that sets you apart from the average. No person aware of their royalty will knowingly live, love, or receive low. It's not in them to do so because it clashes with their rank. I'm telling you, you are too powerful to love low. Prayerfully, your eyes are beginning to open as your view shifts upward.

Have you noticed that nothing I've discussed so far has anything to do with how others see you but how you see yourself through God's lens? He loves you so much that He freely gave you His son. He loves you so much that He shared His name, likeness, and Kingdom. Until a man offers such, he's not the one. Although this is not a relationship book per se, it details some of the common frustrations that women of God experience during their dating journey. Just know that you can't always help who you attract but can help who you entertain. And who you entertain is usually directly correlated with how you see yourself. You entertain and love on the level of the conviction of your rank. You are too powerful to love low.

Don't get me wrong, many of us are playing catch-up, and we're just realizing our worth. Just know that by mere birth, you are worthy, and by the blood of Jesus, you have the right to enforce your worth. Don't be embarrassed if you are in your thirties and beyond and you're just getting it together. God sees all that you've encountered and what has tripped you up along the way. He understands that you were not taught about worth or, quite possibly, your worth was contaminated when you were violated, or maybe your mother mistreated you and your father abandoned you. Perhaps it was the taunts from misguided peers or the cruelty of hateful relatives that robbed your confidence account. Maybe your boyfriend humiliated you by cheating on you, or the broken engagement wounded your soul in ways you can't express. Did your husband walking out on you crush your self-love? Dang it, the call from the other woman exposed your already tormenting thoughts that you were not enough. Maybe it's the weight gain or how low you've gone to feel some degree of "I matter." I can relate. And as

I write, I'm being ministered to as well. However, let's promise that no matter how tough this book gets, acknowledge, confront, and deal with your truth. Cry it out. Yell it out. Make the call. Do whatever it takes as long as you get it out and allow your life to improve. Accept in your mind and heart that you are too powerful to love low.

It Costs to Rank Higher

The problem many Christians face is that the only benefits they desire are prosperity and salvation. They don't want to abide by the code of ethics that details how a woman or man of God should live. And sadly, you wouldn't know that they are believers unless you ran into them at church or they told you. Believe it or not, some Christian women have told me that they aren't interested in ascending higher in God. They desire a man but don't necessarily want or need a Kingdom man. At first, I was insulted by their mindset until I stopped and weighed the fact that it costs to rank higher in God, and not everyone is interested in paying that type of price.

It's true not everyone desires spiritual wealth in their relationships. The sad reality is that they don't realize the root of their willingness to accept a subpar relationship. Even so, that's a topic that's reserved for my students. Joyfully, the number of women who desire Kingdom marriages is plenteous. Most of them are recovering "low-loving" addicts. Therefore, this book is primarily for my Kingdom-minded sisters who desire the culture of God to show up in their relationships for His glory and the changing of their story. In the previous chapter, I addressed the three areas where all believers are equally ranked. However, in the following few chapters, I would like to explore some of the ways that separate us and cause some to rank higher in God while others make no notable progress in their spiritual walk.

Relationship & Intimacy

Some professed Christians operate independently without God. They are believers with their mouths but don't believe they can vibe higher and win in God. They believe in miracles, the finished works of the cross, and that they are essential to God. However, there is a disconnect regarding the personalization and relevancy of God to their lives. For example, they believe in what God did for Moses, Daniel, and even their coworker, but somehow believe that God wouldn't intervene in their lives as He did for said people. Their psyche tells them that God is figurative and impersonal. They have adopted the mentality that the best God has for them is in heaven, and living defeated lives is a part of their cross to bear that will one day lead them to the cross that He, ironically, already bore for them. They have difficulty understanding that God knows their names and desires to commune with them. They secretly admire and some envy or become jealous of those who hear and receive from God. They can't relate because their connection is superficial. They do church check-ins but neglect prayer and Bible study. These individuals are usually dismissive of God and only seek Him in crisis. Either way, they are missing out on a beautiful and thrilling relationship of intimacy with Him. They don't realize how approachable, fun, and pleasant God is. Individuals in a relationship with God are in higher rank brackets than those who aren't. They are more likely to get their prayers answered and freely worship God because they approach God boldly and with confidence. They understand how loved they are and that it pleases God to give them the desires of their hearts according to His will.

Void of Relationship

To date someone void of a relationship with God when you are in relationship with Him is a prime example of loving low and inviting unnecessary turmoil into your life. It's careless and can lead to the non-relational person envying your authentic connection with God. Such an individual will often attempt to insult and minimize your faith and walk with God or take a very passive stance regarding anything spiritual. If you are genuinely connected to God, the disparity in rank will affect you. You will connect with others who love God just as much as you do while leaving your lover out. And no, I am not saying they aren't good men; they just aren't Godly. There is also such a thing as partnering with a good Christian man who isn't Kingdom. He's a believer but not a Kingdom believer. Believe it or not, even this connection is an unexamined example of loving below your rank in God. A lot of Christian women find themselves in such positions for a plethora of reasons. They lost the fight with patience and forfeited the arrival of their Kingdom man for premature settlement.

The above examples may be okay for some, but God designed you to partner with a man who provides and covers well. A man to whom you can relate spiritually. How tragic to share every aspect of your life except your love for God. How sad to give your whole self to a man who hasn't given his entire self to God. To partner with an individual who has the heart of God and can hear God as you do is fire and Kingdom. If you aspire to wear the title of Kingdom, having such a person in your life is necessary. Spiritually speaking, you don't have to be on the same paragraph, but you do need to be on the same page.

I know that most of us grew up in families where the men did not operate as reliable spiritual coverings. For too many of God's covenant-keeping daughters, the idea of dating and marrying a man who loves God as much as they do is unfathomable. Even so, it is what their hearts truly desire. Let no one tell you that entering into covenant with a covenant-keeping man of God is unimportant. It is meaningful, necessary, and beneficial to the Kingdom of God and your destiny. Kingdom marriages are rare, but God desires to make them the standard and norm.

Case Study 1

Janet communicated that when she met her fiancé, she asked him if he believed in Jesus, and he responded, "Absolutely." She was instantly sold. They started attending church together, and she was extremely excited because she prayed for a man with whom she could share her love for God. However, as time progressed, she noticed that he never talked about God or mentioned having Bible study or a life of prayer. She mistakenly equated belief in God with a relationship with God. She neither looked nor asked deep enough. When she brought up spiritual topics, he appeared spiritually dumb. And anytime she mentioned her observation, he replied, "My walk is personal, and everybody can't be on the same spiritual level as you." As time progressed, he began making sly remarks that she inserted God into everything as if she couldn't do anything on her own. He said such because her fondness for God assured that His name was often mentioned in conversations. She always gave Him glory for His assistance in her life.

As more time went on, she began to detect that he was jealous of her love for God and her ability to hear His voice through the Holy

Spirit. Her broken inner child was willing to compromise because she didn't want him to abandon her. She didn't want to lose the attention that she was getting. So, the grown woman within bowed to her inner child's fear of loneliness and stopped talking about God as much. She wanted to make him feel more comfortable, so she exalted him so he could feel like a man capable of leading her spiritually. She went out of her way to make him feel assured that nothing was wrong with his non-relationship with God.

Presently, he attends church with her, and the only spiritual authority he exudes is when it comes to saying grace over their meals 😊. Within the two years of their relationship, he hasn't progressed spiritually. They now live together, and she's pregnant. Her unaddressed soul wounds (fear of rejection and loneliness) blinded her. Unfortunately, she doesn't see anything wrong with their connection. When I brought her life of compromise to her attention, she snapped, "It works for us." Sure, it does if she's looking for a connection void of Kingdom. When you truly experience God, you may be able to show out for a season, but you'll never be able to rest in that season. She's powerful, but unfortunately, she chose to love low in exchange for company.

This type of connection can work very well if both individuals do not have a personal relationship with Christ because they are equally ranked. If she marries this man, she will marry below her rank in God, and time will expose the cost of her compromise. What a spiritual shame that she won't be able to share her very intimate love for God with the man she loves unless he changes. For now, she's treading in dangerous waters. It's obvious she's not heeding the counsel of the Holy Spirit that she's unequally yoked. Although her broken inner child will say otherwise, neither marriage nor a child can make a wrong connection right. You cannot marry someone lukewarm in God and remain hot in God and hot for them. Indeed, one of the relationships will suffer. In this case, it's evident which.

Yes To The Call

A quick way to gain rank in the realm of the spirit is by saying yes to the call of God on your life and walking it out. Ironically, you can know what you're called to and still say no because you're not willing to pay the price that accompanies the call. For example, I pay a very hefty price for saying yes to being a deliverance minister. I mean, you should hear me trying to describe what I do to potential suitors. It's an attraction killer 😁. This upset me when my eyes were low, and I loved low. I now know that the opposite effect will happen for the right one. The anointing and a woman operating in her purpose are sexy! And yes, I said the word sexy!

When you live a purposeful life, you have no choice but to thrive and live a fulfilled life because the blessings and power of God show up where His will is on display. However, operating in your God-ordained purpose comes with many sacrifices, and you must be healed enough to rock them out without becoming resentful. Embracing your purpose is not always popular, and it isn't always comfortable. It is a big deal to operate boldly and efficiently in your purpose. It usually demands significant risks and displays of great faith.

Wandering Without Purpose

Many people are wandering around without purpose. They are in fields, including ministry areas, that are unsuitable for them. The fear of failure and rejection stifles others, so they avoid what their soul is attracted to. They never rise; they play low and safe. When people are in the right place and position, they are in miracle territory for extraordinary things to happen. They are in a position to change and impact lives. They live fulfilled and are ranked on an elevated level. God never intended for any of us to wander. He's too intentional for that. One last point: do not underestimate the jealousy and hate that operating in your purpose will attract. Your placement is torture to those who are out of alignment. They are not where they are supposed to be. Their souls cannot rest, and as a result, they disturb your rest.

Partnering Low

To partner with someone who does not know their purpose is another example of loving low. I must add that loving low doesn't always mean the relationship will be rocky, abusive, or non-productive. It simply means that God can't get his highest level of glory from the connection. Think about having a plate of the best hot wings on the planet. You appreciate the art of wing-making. You understand what constitutes stellar wings so much that you eat them to the bone. You leave no meat behind. You get the full glory from those wings. However, you glance over and notice that your partner left so much meat on the bones that you can only conclude that he didn't see or taste the value of the world's most excellent wings. And instead of simmering in what just blessed your taste buds, you expend energy to argue, convince, and motivate him to take his wings more seriously. You may even overindulge by finishing what he left behind. His lack of enthusiasm or understanding risks robbing you of momentum, excitement, and even thankfulness for your wings. And so it is in a relationship where you're unequally yoked in purpose. There is always going to be unchartered meat left behind.

A partner who doesn't know why they are here will drag you down and affect your equilibrium. They will not understand your sacrifices, tears, struggles, faith moves, and risks because they are creators and innovators of nothing. At best, they can celebrate with you, but that will never be enough for a powerful woman who loves high. She's a team player, and she wants her man to walk out his purpose, too! You may be thinking, *as long as they are doing well where they are, it's fine by me.* Possibly so, if you're not yet Kingdom-minded. Jesus was a great carpenter, but it was not his purpose to be a carpenter. What if he would have stopped at carpentry? Remember, success in the natural doesn't always equate to success in the spirit realm.

Case Study 2

Like me, Tonya is a social worker specializing in inner healing and deliverance. She was being courted by a Kingdom man who did not understand the ministry of deliverance. To make matters more complicated, he wasn't operating in his purpose. Tony was a medical doctor because his family pressured him to choose the medical field. His true calling was in the area of auto mechanics. He could fix any vehicle effortlessly, and he loved it. However, he knew that operating in his gift would cause him much grief with his family and, especially his parents, who are retired physicians. His little boy within craved his family's validation and affirmation. Therefore, he settled for the path of least resistance. Truthfully, although it was easy for him, he hated medical school. His Residency experience was a complete nightmare. Although excellent in his field, he was miserable entertaining patients all day. Tonya observed that he was at peace and happiest whenever he was fixing or talking about cars. He instantly became a chatterbox and inspiring as he shared his passion for cars.

Tony loved Tonya but got irritated by her love for her profession. He didn't understand how she could be so happy getting paid what he called crumbs. He didn't appreciate her dedication to her clients and tried to downplay deliverance by saying she was doing more social work than anything else. He admired her but was ashamed of her purpose and tried to avoid discussing her profession with his colleagues, family, and friends. Tonya admitted that she, too, began to downplay her gift to please him until God told her that she had to choose between serving Him or dating Tony. Although Tony was making good money, loved her, and was honestly a good person, he behaved like an enemy to her purpose. Although Tony had potential, his lack of understanding placed powerful-Tonya in the loving low category because he fragmented her.

One morning, while getting ready for work, God spoke to Tonya's heart in the midst of her conversing with her broken inner child. God reminded her that He raised her and pushed her through too much mud to allow a mortal and flawed man to cause her to become ashamed of her purpose. Feeling exposed and convicted, Tonya decided to shut her inner child down and trust God. She ended the relationship. Her determination to put God first woke Tony up, to her surprise and God's glory. He did not want to lose her, so he probed to understand what led to her decision. Tonya's willingness to prioritize her purpose and walk away from such a great catch (in his eyes) stunned him and made him seek God for answers. He knew that Tonya was wife material and contained his favor. Instead of giving up, he entered a season of prayer and fasting. In that place, he came face to face with God and himself. In God's presence, he could not escape the truth that he was not living out his God-designed purpose. He surrendered to God and won Tonya back. Within the year, he left the medical field and pursued various certifications in auto mechanics.

Tony pursued knowledge to understand deliverance better and fell in love with Tonya's purpose. He reignited his relationship with Tonya with a renewed mind. He allowed her to walk him through deliverance, and his entire life opened up. His parents eventually came around and encouraged him to open an auto mechanics shop and dealership specializing in specialty cars. He and Tonya got married, and he helped her open a practice in the heartbeat of downtown Atlanta, Georgia. Ironically, she ended up walking his entire family through deliverance. Today, with their combined efforts, they make almost four times as much as they did when Tony operated outside his purpose. They brought elevation, settlement, and favor into each other's lives.

Self-Love

Do you realize how you see, accept, and love yourself affects your rank in God? Without a healthy self-outlook, you will struggle to deem yourself worthy of receiving God's grace, mercy, love, and best for your life. Your level of self-love affects how you approach God and view the relevance of His promises to your life. Self-love is so important that in Matthew 22:36-39, Jesus informed one of his followers (who inquired about the greatest commandment in the law) that loving God with all was number one, followed by loving your neighbor as you love yourself. Undoubtedly, self-love is a crucial ingredient in loving God and others. So much so that it's not optional to love yourself; it's a command. God is not a fan of watching his children love low, and that includes themselves.

The challenge is that many people spend their lives trying to love others while their self-love is on the floor. That type of love always becomes perverted, and I'm not just speaking romantically. This is equally applicable to casual, family, and friend relationships. The quest to love without self-love is low love. It's usually laced with unspoken expectations and a twisted desire to be affirmed and validated by others. It is perverted to expect others to value you or give to you what you don't value or give to yourself. God help us all if their unspoken desires are unmet, attitudes fester, resentment builds, and damage to the person's already low self-perception increases. God never meant for his creation to operate in a state of confusion regarding their value. God designed it so another flawed human cannot convict you of your worth. You must connect to the originator of the creation for such insight. When this step is skipped, people will love themselves and others from a low place. On the outside, you may not be able to tell, but boy oh boy, when the lights go out, and the silence ensues, mind torment prevails.

Self-Hate

Far too many try to love God without loving themselves. Through the portals of time, this, too, proves disastrous and perverted. You'd be surprised to discover who's aggressively professing Christ while feeling let down and forgotten by Him. They perform for Him, but they don't feel loved by Him. They understand the concept that Abba loves them, and they are royalty. However, it's head and not heart knowledge. They try to love and serve him with their all while harboring self-hate. These souls try to perform their way into God's love without understanding it's freely given. They mistakenly believe that it's God's love that they are trying to earn when it's their own. Their foundational blows of rejection and abandonment have left wounds that skew how they see and love themselves. They need healing. Until then, they will continue harboring self-hate and loving themselves low. Psychologically speaking, they believe that God sees them as they see themselves—unworthy. And if He sees them as worthy, they see themselves as worthy.

Projecting Self-Hate

Too many of God's daughters harbor self-hate and, in turn, project it onto others—especially other women. A prime example is how many women struggled to congratulate and celebrate Kamala Harris, the country's first black, female, Asian American Vice President. Instead of celebrating her, some women chose to pick her apart; just like they picked themselves apart. They couldn't celebrate with her because her accomplishment exposed a broken place within. You don't have to subscribe to a person's values to recognize and honor a historical moment. One monkey may not be able to stop a show, but a wounded inner child most certainly can.

Allow Your Soul To Speak

You may be reading this and thinking, *yes, I love myself,* but do you truly? Dressing, living, driving well, and getting your hair, nails, makeup, and lashes done is self-care but isn't necessarily self-love. How do you feel about yourself without those things? Do you accept yourself unconditionally? How do you treat your body? Do you have healthy boundaries? How do you talk to and about yourself? What are your silent thoughts like? Go deep. Go to the root and allow your soul to speak. She will tell you the truth.

What I love about Jesus is that he's a foundational teacher. He gets to the core of matters. Ladies, this is where you must start in the healing process. You must examine how you truly feel about God and how you truly feel about yourself. And once you do, examine what damaged your God and self-perceptions and minister to those places. This is what I help men and women from all around the world do. I help them heal their foundations so their inner child can be free. A healed woman is attractive, unstoppable, and walks gracefully, making others feel wonderful and inspired in her company.

Case Study 3

Terrell and Brandi were high school sweethearts who married straight out of school. Terrell entered the military, and Brandi enrolled in a nursing program at the local community college. For the first year of their marriage, Brandi did ok within the marriage but struggled because of Terrell's extended absences. She found being alone challenging even though she understood he was working on his career and was wholly devoted to her. Instead of focusing on school and building a home, as time went on, she began to hang out with some of her friends that she made in the community. She became a busybody. Resting and silence terrorized her. She was great whenever Terrell was at home and showering her with attention. However, she fell apart whenever deployment hit their house and couldn't go.

She finished her nursing degree and found fulfillment and pride in becoming an RN. Over time, she started spending out of control on things that accentuated her looks. Her careful attention to her appearance began attracting attention she had never received. This drove her to crank things up. Her social media pages went from highlighting the modest Brandi to hosting daily racy photoshoots. Amazed by her transformation, the likes started pouring in. The attention satisfied her until it didn't. Brandi eventually became depressed and started dabbling with different narcotics after being introduced by another military spouse.

When Terrell came home from Korea, he found his wife in bad shape. The house was unkempt, several bills were outstanding, and Brandi had lost weight. It was obvious that she was a user, and Terrell confronted her. She admitted her state, and he was devastated by her drug use and other cries for attention. He immediately asked for military leave to address his home issues. He encouraged Brandi to resign from her nursing position before her drug addiction was exposed and caused her to lose her license. He wasn't sure what to do next, so he contacted his chain of command, who directed him to the military Chaplain, who then recommended counseling and private drug rehab. They followed his counsel and, over time, emerged stronger than ever.

In this particular case, Brandi was blessed to have a very mature and supportive spouse. Her story ran the risk of spiraling out of control. In counseling, it was revealed that Brandi lacked self-love and was suffering from chronic rejection and abandonment issues grounded in the story of abuse suffered at the hands of her parents. It was her broken inner child who was afraid of being alone and needed constant validation to feel worthy. She drove Brandi to subconsciously make Terrell her god. All was well as long as she could drown her self-hate in his love and attention. She made him her world, and when she couldn't, she fell apart and looked for other means to satisfy the holes in her soul.

Terrell had to come to grips with his part in the story. He knew that she was broken, but her dependency made him feel valued. He became her enabler and answer. He learned this behavior as a child when he became his alcoholic mom's caregiver and protector. Acting as god was familiar to him. Brandi desperately needed to be rescued, and he desperately needed someone to take care of him. They both came to realize that they were giving each other low love. By God's grace, they both realized they were too powerful to love low. In their case, it was discovered that their love was genuinely authentic after exposing and healing their brokenness. Truthfully, this is not the case for many couples whose dysfunctions drew them together. Terrell and Brandi joined a spirit-filled church where they learned to embrace God as Abba's father. Submission to the finished works of the cross, soaked in the conviction of self-love, became their new foundation.

That Girl's On Fire

A fire-filled life usually separates the girls from the women of God. This is where a decision has been made to live in purpose for God in every aspect of one's life. This individual is sold out for God in the most radical and beautiful way. Communing with God through prayer and Bible study is her delight. Her speech glorifies God. She's wholesome in her attire. She's either saving her body for her husband or rocking the status of a born-again virgin. She's careful about her witness, and repentance is her pleasure. Specific environments are not worthy of her presence. Certain conversations caused her to exit stage left. She's careful regarding the quality of music that enters her eargates. She's confident in her God and isn't afraid of the world's rejection. Her home is a place where God is always welcome. She doesn't mind admitting fault and apologizing to set things right. Her little girl within is healed and in check. She desires to be righteous over being right. She avoids gossip and looks for ways to be a blessing. Laughter fills her heart. She knows when to war and when to rest. She is decided. Her need for validation and affirmation flows from within and above. She is not above correction and healing. Deliverance is her portion. She's quick to forgive. She's honest. She prays for her God-ordained spouse. She's patient and kind. She knows she's not perfect and doesn't feel the need to be perfect. She's in love with one man, God. Her walk with God is sure and consistent. This is the highest rank possible because she is on fire.

Spiritual Suicide

For such a woman to partner with a man who is not ranked on that same level is spiritual suicide. He will demand that she compromise to complement his lukewarm life. Ironically, the fire will initially attract him, but when he weighs the cost and decides not to pay it, he despises her fire and attempts to bring her down to his level. If unsuccessful, he will abandon or stay and torment her. This woman cannot date as the world and even as other Christians date. Her mate has to be handpicked and delivered by God.

This woman is not as rare as she may sound. However, she is often criticized and mislabeled as a Christian fanatic or plain Jane. The world despises her and looks for ways to pervert her. If her suitor is not ranked as high as she is, he will seek to pervert her and strip her of her confidence with his subtle suggestions for improvement. Her willingness to please will sometimes knock her off course. The marital wait for such a woman can seem long because Daddy can't trust her heart and life with just anyone. This woman can, over time, fall into the trap of seeing the wait as rejection versus protection. Her warfare is thick, and it will take a general in the spirit to protect and cover her as a husband should. While others can play with whom they marry, her husband has to love her as Christ loves the church.

Case Study 4

When Jerry met Marcy, it was love at first sight. Instantly, he knew he wanted to marry her, so he prayed and fasted about it. He could not believe that a woman of her caliber was still single. In passing, he knew that Marcy found him attractive and was somewhat interested based on her body language. To his disappointment, she was not moved with outward excitement when he approached her with his desire. Rejection tried to shut down his confidence, but the Holy Spirit raised it. Jerry sought God regarding Marcy's nonchalant response, and the Holy Spirit communicated that Marcy had settled within herself that she was not desirable and marriage was not her portion. She was sincerely at rest with the conclusion.

Marcy is lovely, so attracting men was never a problem for her. However, when she decided to become serious about God, the different men who came into her life told her that she needed to relax her personality and zeal for God. They said this because she was clear and vocal about her Christian convictions. She wanted a genuine commitment and to marry before starting a family. Her friends laughed at her vow of celibacy and told her that she needed some sex in her life to loosen her up. Her mother suggested she wear lashes, hair extensions, and tighter-fitting clothing to snatch one of Atlanta's most eligible bachelors. Aunt Sadie told her that men of God no longer desired seriously saved women.

Everyone wanted to hang around Marcy as long as she checked her spirituality at the door. She was naturally funny and pleasant. She tried repeatedly to blend in, but the Holy Spirit always interrupted the fun to get his point across. Marcy loved being used by God and enjoyed her life to the fullest. She danced, laughed, and traveled often. However, she got tired of the criticism and carnal advice and decided to distance herself from family and friends who couldn't appreciate her fire. Marcy agreed she would not allow another man to tear her down. She recognized the assignment of the enemy, which was to send men into her life who told her that she was not carnal enough. She wasn't angry but determined to keep God as her focus.

Jerry could relate because he, too, was criticized for his fire. He was called weird and gay because he didn't chase skirts or hang with the carnal men in his environment. He lived a consecrated life. While in prayer, the Holy Spirit told Jerry to tell Marcy, "I don't want to change anything about you but your last name." Ha! That phrase stopped her in her tracks and instantly unlocked her heart. Nine months later, they were married and are now in their sixth year. She put the Kingdom first, and God placed her husband into her hands. What repelled the wrong ones drew the right one. How powerful and anointed are the couples who fight fire for fire and love on their in God!

You Are Kingdom

Dearest reader, it's time for you to locate yourself in the realm of the spirit and examine where you're ranked. Be honest with yourself. If you don't like what you see, you have the freedom and power to choose a higher level. This is on you, so put your thumb down because no one will rescue you from your stuck place. Therefore, give yourself full permission to rescue yourself.

How you show up for yourself in this world is important and indicative of how bright your future will be. Becoming the best version of yourself is God's will for your life. Ask yourself, does God's version of me match my version of me? Yeah, you have work to do. We all do. May I suggest elevating to your highest possible self is your reasonable service? Elevation is for you and only you. Still, others will benefit from you showing up in life, LARGE, and yes, that includes your Kingdom man. He will be drawn to your light, so No More playing small.

Size Five Shoes

God blew my mind a few months back. I quoted Matthew 6:33 ("But seek ye first the Kingdom of God, and his righteousness; and all these things shall be added unto you.") to him as a legal right to be paired with my Kingdom man. I bargained, "God, I've been busy working for you, so according to your word, I am ready to have my Kingdom man added to my life." Lovingly, God educated me that his children often quote Matthew 6:33 without realizing that the Kingdom of God is a culture with many extensions. The Kingdom is distinct in sound and movement. God responded, "Faithe, seeking the Kingdom is not about being busy with ministry. The Kingdom should be sought after and reflected in every area of your life." The conversation didn't last long, but I got the point. The Kingdom should show up in our health, relationships, finances, speech, profession, and emotions. I had never thought of it in such a manner, and I knew that I had more work to do.

I don't know about you, but this perspective challenged me and appealed to my already-held conviction that marriage is not the most incredible blessing or highest achievement that God has for me. I decided to say goodbye to the size five shoes I had been forced to embrace my size fifteen feet. This day, I challenge and beg you to renounce your size five mentality and say hello to your proper size. Initially, rocking your adequate size will be uncomfortable. Pain is associated with undoing the damage caused by scrunching your mind into too small places. Hang in there because the reward is so much greater than the pain of damage reversal. You are kingdom and too powerful to love low!

Trade Your Cross For Your Crown

I called Calvin to finalize the transfer of our property to him. After agreeing to all of his terms, he spewed words of uncertainty aimed at unearthing my peace. Y'all, my spiritual ears heightened at that moment and zoomed into the signal of something dark. I saw the assignment for what it was. I realized that I was dealing with a borderline narcissistic personality fueled by a demon named Leviathan. For weeks, Calvin made my life a living hell by insisting on what he was and wasn't going to do concerning severing ties. And when I finally became tired of trying to flex my will, I found peace and decided to agree to everything, and what do you know, he flipped the script! He was accustomed to manipulating my emotions with passive-aggressive behaviors. I was such an easy target to trigger. However, the Holy Spirit was over it and exposed what was using him.

Without hesitation, I yelled, "You nasty demon. I see you for who you are. I hear you, Leviathan. All of these years, it's been you that I've been contending with, and I'm over it. You can't have my peace." Readers, I slammed the phone down and warred like I had lost my mind. I laughed and cried at the realization that I had allowed a dark spirit to take me down through there! Here's the thing: I used to tell him I heard Leviathan in his voice, but I was too close to the situation to fight effectively. Too many compromises took place for me to be a serious contender. Once I realized what I was dealing with, my confidence shot to ten, and I moved in faith.

Calvin was not ready for the arrows that I shot at him. I no longer saw him as strong and worthy of following. I no longer cared about what his family or friends thought of me. Suddenly, I didn't even care what he thought about me. I was experiencing what the beginning processes of healing could do. In my sight, this once beautiful man was now pitiful to behold. I elevated him way past his rank and undermined mine. How could I miss that it was an honor to capture the attention of Ms. Faithe DesChamps? I was the prize the entire time, but my brokenness flipped the script and made him the pseudo-prize to which I was honored to be connected.

Calvin eventually extended a weak apology for how he treated me. He stated that I hurt him when I told him that I didn't want him. Poor thang became the victim. Anywho, he expressed that it was at that moment he decided he was done. I responded, "I was done when my bare feet hit the cold, wet, and dirty concrete." Looking back, there is no way that I would have recovered emotionally from that night while connected to him. The memory of how he arrogantly left me uncovered would have haunted me. What he did was a grave dishonor. Dishonor is what one attracts when one is loving oneself and others low.

Being the kindhearted woman I am, since he lived in another state, I helped him get things squared away with the property before leaving Alabama. During all of the exchanges, we laughed and shared teamwork moments. I thought for a few seconds that we could make things work. I thought of how deliverance could change errrrrthang back when we were in love. Ha! I meant well in my heart, but hunnies, it was nothing more than the residue of familiarity. The very last conversation that I had with Calvin occurred during my second week in my new residence. We veered into a discussion about him not supporting my ministry when we were together. He sneered that I only wanted his support so that I could brag that I had a man. Yes, once again, I was about to argue with a size five mindset, and I disconnected the phone, never more to look back. I made a permanent decision to choose me. I reminded myself I was too powerful to give and accept low love. I decided it was time to trade my cross for my crown. I was carrying an unnecessary cross. I was too powerful to accept and give low love. I came to my whole self and praised in the revelation that I was free and could now write a check that heaven was willing to cash. I traded in my cross for my crown.

I had won the victory, but not the war. I had someone very special but very broken to face. I had to face my wounded inner child. Whew! Left unattended, she would dismantle and sabotage my forward movement no matter how much everything else was in place. Women of God, take a deep breath and get the Kleenex ready as we closely examine the works and mindset of the broken child within you. She may be your greatest enemy when she should be your closest friend. Grab volume two, relax, and get ready to delve deeper into your healing. In the meantime, Readers, remember that you are too powerful to love low.

The Power Pusher invites you to connect with her on her Facebook, Twitter, and Instagram accounts. For more information regarding upcoming classes, private services, and ministry invites, please visit, The Power Pusher's website: www.thepowerpusher.org

www.ingramcontent.com/pod-product-compliance
Lightning Source LLC
LaVergne TN
LVHW051151080426
835508LV00021B/2574